30119 026 246 55 5

THE MANAGEMENT MODELS POCKETBOOK

D1638554

By Dr Mike Clayton

Drawings by Phil Hailstone

"Invaluable both as a foundation to the subject for new managers and as a quick refresher for more seasoned managers and leaders."
Cryss Mennaceur, Head of Organisational Development, London Borough of Sutton

"If I wanted to know about the essence of leadership or motivational theory, or even just how to communicate more effectively, this is the book I would turn to."
Adam Wynard, Ministry of Justice, Justice Academy

"With so many daily challenges faced by managers, this book is a great way to refresh and enthuse yourself with some great management model thinking – a pocket-sized gem for managers."
Perry Timms, Head of Organisational Development, Big Lottery Fund

Published by:
Management Pocketbooks Ltd
Laurel House, Station Approach, Alresford, Hants SO24 9JH, U.K.
Tel: +44 (0)1962 735573   Fax: +44 (0)1962 733637
E-mail: sales@pocketbook.co.uk
Website: www.pocketbook.co.uk

This edition published 2009.

British Library Cataloguing-in-Publication Data – A catalogue record for this book is available from the British Library.

ISBN 978 1 906610 03 6

Design, typesetting and graphics by **efex ltd**. Printed in U.K.

CONTENTS

GUEST FOREWORD

I met my first management model in about 1965 as a participant on a course based on Blake and Mouton's 'Concern for Task/Concern for People' grid. We spent a week exploring five management styles in depth and I came away convinced that the grid was The Answer. (This was when I was naïve and believed in Answers!). Since then I have come across numerous management models (and even invented some myself!) and learnt how to use them without falling into the trap of expecting them to provide a ready-made Answer.

Management is a complex business. It is rather like having to keep too many plates spinning simultaneously on wobbly bamboo canes. I have always thought of models as a convenient way to simplify complexity so that it becomes possible to prioritise and cut a path through the confusion. The Blake and Mouton model, for example, helped me to understand that there is a time and a place for different management styles.

Ever since this early, formative experience I have been drawn to management models. They appeal to the pragmatist in me. Experience has taught me that models are relatively easy to understand and that things that are understood are likely to be used and that things that are used make a difference (hopefully, for the better!). Appropriate action is always what counts.

I no longer swallow models whole. I prefer to use them as useful starting points and adapt them so that they become 'mine'. It is like taking a ready-made suit and having it altered so that it fits you snugly. Bitter experience has taught me that adaptations can annoy the originators of the model but, so long as they have been properly acknowledged, I don't care. What matters is to develop something that works for you. Models spawn techniques – nice, doable things that you can cling to as you become skilled. When a model stops short of offering ready-made, practical techniques, that's good; it provides you with an opportunity to fill in the gaps and make it your own. The sequence is: take a model; distil it into techniques you can use; test the techniques in practice; review and refine; keep practising until you become skilled. (I can feel another model coming on!)

So, I have no hesitation in commending this delightful pocketbook to you; ten promising starting points just waiting for you to cherry pick and turn them into something that helps you become an even better manager.

Dr Peter Honey, April 2009

AUTHOR'S INTRODUCTION

'There is nothing so practical as a good theory.' Kurt Lewin

Models are an important aid in effective management. They give us a way to simplify the world enough so that we can understand what we observe and predict what will happen. But an effective model must not simplify so much that valuable subtlety is lost. All models have descriptive power but each has its own strengths; it can fulfil one or more of the three principal purposes of models:

- Explanation: helping us understand what is
- Prediction: helping us anticipate what will be
- Process: helping us create a reliable outcome

This pocketbook presents ten valuable models. Each one can help you to learn and develop your management practice. As the saying goes, *'all models are wrong'*, but a good one is useful, while remaining simple. I believe these ten all achieve that balance.

This book is dedicated to Felicity and Sophia.

LEADING
PEOPLE AT WORK

1 Leadership Continuum

2 Action Centred Leadership

3 Tuckman's Group Development:
Forming, Storming, Norming,
Performing

THE PROBLEM

Many managers take on leadership roles without the chance to prepare adequately. Do you know what is expected of you as a leader? If you do, how will you achieve it? Many leadership models are immensely helpful. They focus on either:

- Traits: personality and character traits that make a 'good leader'
- Styles: behaviours that support 'good leadership'
- Roles: the things a 'good leader' needs to do

'Some are born great, some achieve greatness, and some have greatness thrust upon them.'

William Shakespeare

Models based on traits: Personality Leadership

Earliest thinking focused on traits. People thought that leadership was an innate ability – one you were born with …or not. This is the so-called 'Great Man' theory. At the very least, your personality formed early in your life. Therefore, this approach does not suggest that leadership can be learned when you need it. Fortunately, more recent thinking has created practical models of leadership that you can learn, practise and refine. Leadership is accessible to everyone.

LEADING PEOPLE AT WORK

THE PROBLEM

Models based on styles: Situational Leadership
People have different strengths and lead in different ways. Some models look at different leadership styles and suggest which situations require which types of leader. Others show you how to use a range of styles and choose, according to circumstances. Both approaches are known as situational leadership. Use the first when recruiting a leader to fill a particular role. The second approach offers ways a leader can get the best out of people, by focusing on two main skills:

- Sensing the needs of the situation
- Being able to adapt your style accordingly

Tannenbaum and Schmidt's Leadership Continuum is a situational leadership model, offering a range of styles and ways to select among them.

Models based on roles: Functional Leadership
The problem is that neither personality nor situational models of leadership describe what you need to do, as a leader. This is what functional models offer. They answer the question most new leaders ask: *'What am I supposed to do?'* Action Centred Leadership is a functional model. It says your role is to meet the needs of your team.

1 LEADERSHIP CONTINUUM

THE PROBLEM

Is there a right way and a wrong way to lead people? Management thinkers have been debating this for years. In the 1930s, Kurt Lewin, with others, examined the effectiveness of three styles:

- Autocratic – I'll tell you what to do
- Democratic – I'll work with you
- Laissez-faire – I'll leave you to it

Their conclusions were that, while each has its merits, democratic leadership was most effective and created the highest levels of morale. Laissez-faire leadership produced the poorest results. The biggest critique of this work was that Lewin and his colleagues were working with children!

> 'Today's manager is more likely to deal with employees who resent being treated as subordinate.'
>
> **Robert Tannenbaum and Warren H Schmidt**

What about the workplace?

For a manager in the workplace, you have a number of concerns to balance when deciding on a leadership style. Most managers cannot help thinking that there must be a *'right way'* to do things – if only they can find it.

1 LEADERSHIP CONTINUUM

THE PROBLEM

In distinguishing the 'right way' from the 'wrong way', managers often express a number of concerns. Here are six that come up frequently:

- *'How do I get the best results from my team?'*
  I want them to work together and collaborate, harnessing everyone's capabilities
- *'How do I get the best results from each individual?'*
  No two people are the same, so how can I please all of my people all of the time?
- *'How do I keep my people motivated?*
  I want a happy and enthusiastic workforce so what's the best way to treat them?
- *'How much should I use the power I have?'*
  Some people like to be told what to do and anyway, I'm in charge: I carry the can
- *'How much should I delegate?'*
  Which decisions should I make myself, and which should my team make?
- *'How should I adapt to the culture of my team or my organisation?'*
  The prevailing culture will influence people's expectations of leadership

All of these concerns, and more, will bother a manager who wants to do right by their team and get the best possible results.

QUICK SUMMARY

In their 1958 Harvard Business Review article, Robert Tannenbaum and Warren H Schmidt set out a range of leadership behaviours. They set out seven distinct stages on a continuum, which vary from telling team members their decision, through selling their idea and consulting on the problem, to handing over decision-making. Equally valuable is their assessment of how a manager can decide how to lead and choose which of the styles will work best. They offer three considerations:

- **Forces in the manager** – your values and style, and your assessment of the risk
- **Forces in the team members** – your assessment of their readiness and enthusiasm to assume responsibility
- **Forces in the situation** – time pressure, the group's effectiveness, organisational culture

A re-published version, in 1973, includes the authors' retrospective commentary. This pocketbook includes some of their later ideas.

The Leadership Continuum is a major foundation for situational leadership, and the two trademarked models developed by Paul Hersey and Kenneth Blanchard.

QUICK SUMMARY

Continuum of Leadership Behaviour:
Seven degrees of management authority and team member freedom

'Authoritarian Leadership'
Use of authority by manager

'Democratic Leadership'
Freedom for team members to lead

The manager

The situation

The team members

A range of behaviours from the purely authoritarian *'Manager makes a decision and announces it'* through five intermediate styles, to the most democratic *'Manager allows group to make a decision'* within appropriate constraints.

The manager, the team members and the situation each influence the choice of style.

THE SEVEN BEHAVIOURS

Manager makes the decision and announces it
With no opportunity for the group to participate, this is a purely authoritarian style of leadership, with no consideration to other points of view. Perhaps this is at its most appropriate in a crisis. The manager will set clear instructions and expectations.

Manager 'sells' their decision
Here too, the manager takes on the role of decision-maker but, to limit resistance, acts as an advocate for their decision by focusing on the benefits to the group. This is valuable when your decision is not for debate, but you need the group's support.

Manager presents their decision and invites questions
Once again, the manager is in control, but now allows the group to explore their ideas to better understand the decision. The manager has become, in a small way, accountable to their team, but without committing to take account of their opinions.

Manager presents a tentative decision, subject to change
Now the group's opinions can count. The manager retains the role of identifying and resolving the problem, but consults their team before finalising the decision. While the team can contribute, the manager retains ultimate decision-making authority.

THE SEVEN BEHAVIOURS

Manager presents the problem, gets suggestions and then makes a decision
The manager still retains ultimate decision-making authority but now shares responsibility for finding the solution with the group. The team therefore feels able to make suggestions that will really influence the final decision. The manager does not pre-judge the solution, and capitalises upon the group's knowledge and insights.

Manager defines the limits within which the group makes the decision
Now decision-making sits with the team. The manager retains responsibility for defining the problem and, significantly, setting operational boundaries. These may include constraints upon the final decision. This is delegation, although the manager may wish to be a part of the group. In this case, they will not seek any disproportionate influence, arising from their status.

Manager allows group to make decision, subject to organisational constraints
The group has as much freedom as the manager can grant them. The group's limits come from a higher level than the manager. Again, the manager may assist the group and commits to respect their decision.

1 LEADERSHIP CONTINUUM

WHICH STYLE?

FORCES IN THE MANAGER

Tannenbaum and Schmidt identify four principal forces in the manager that will influence their choice of leadership behaviour:

Values – Your attitude to management; the extent to which you believe people should share decision-making or that you should carry the burden of leadership alone.

Inclinations – Your personal style will also influence your choice of behaviour: are you naturally inclined to be directive or collaborative?

Confidence – How much trust do you have in the people who work for you? And, indeed, how much trust do you have in yourself?

Security – In an uncertain situation, control gives a sense of security. So how much control do you need, to feel comfortable with the uncertainty? Making the decision yourself creates certainty.

1 LEADERSHIP CONTINUUM

WHICH STYLE?
FORCES IN THE TEAM MEMBERS

Tannenbaum and Schmidt suggest that a range of conditions dictate your attitude towards trusting the group with a decision. You will consider group members':

- Need for independence
- Readiness to assume responsibility
- Comfort or discomfort with ambiguity
- Interest in the problem
- Assessment of the problem's importance
- Understanding of and sympathy for the organisation's goals
- Relevant knowledge and experience
- Expectations towards participating in decision-making
- Trust for you, as a manager

Where you feel able to delegate responsibility, you will also be making a statement about your trust in the group. This can have a profound effect on the group's motivation.

WHICH STYLE?

FORCES IN THE SITUATION

As well as considering yourself, and your assessment of your followers, Tannenbaum and Schmidt provide four situational considerations that will influence your style of leadership.

Organisation – The culture of your organisation will influence your team's expectations and the effectiveness of different styles. Group size, sensitivity of the task and physical logistics, for example, can all be relevant.

Group effectiveness – How well does the group work together? What is their track record and how do you assess their potential? Good group decision-making needs diversity of perspective and a willingness to listen, to share, and to evaluate ideas openly.

Time pressure – Group decision-making takes time. Under pressure, a rapid and authoritarian decision is sometimes needed.

The problem itself – Some problems dictate the decision process: where does the expertise sit? With you, alone, or distributed among your team?

HOW GOOD IS THE LEADERSHIP CONTINUUM?

Tannenbaum and Schmidt describe their model's principal strengths in their commentary on the model. They assert that it:

- Is useful in a wide variety of organisations
- Sanctions a wide range of behaviour
- Helps managers to analyse their own behaviour

It also guides you in your choice of style and is entirely complementary with other effective leadership models, such as Adair's Action Centred Leadership.

It is hard to find a genuine criticism of this model. There are certainly things it doesn't do, such as indicate how to sell, consult or delegate a decision, but this hardly seems a fair criticism. Likewise, in formulating their three forces, the authors necessarily assume that the manager has sufficient information to make a choice. The perennial criticism of any model is that it over simplifies. While this argument may be levelled at later situational leadership models, Tannenbaum and Schmidt offer a wide array of options and considerations.

So, in summary, this is not a good model, this is a very good model.

VARIATIONS ON A THEME
LINKS TO OTHER MODELS IN THIS BOOK

- **Action Centred Leadership** is a model of the roles of a leader. It complements this model's approach to deciding how to discharge some of those roles

- The Leadership Continuum is about when to use authority. The **Power Bases** model sets out where your authority comes from. Tannenbaum and Schmidt focused on 'legitimate power'. Other power bases can make your leadership more successful and you can strengthen your power bases by your choice of leadership style

- Tuckman's model of **Group Development** will support you in assessing the group's readiness to assume responsibility. It is also true that your choice of leadership style may advance or slow the rate of group formation

- Where a group expects responsibility and does not get it, the frustration can lead to demotivation. Where they feel ill-prepared for the responsibility you give them, the fear of failure can demotivate. And when you ask more of the group with little or no reward, morale will fall. This is Vroom's **Expectancy Theory** in a nutshell

LEARN MORE

The original article, with the authors' retrospective commentary, is available as an HBR Classic, in a reprint from the Harvard Business Review.

- *How to Choose a Leadership Pattern*, Robert Tannenbaum and Warren H Schmidt, Harvard Business Review, May-June 1973

Learn about other, related models and ideas

There are two proprietary models of situational leadership on the market, each with a rich set of resources. To find out more, look up:
- Situational Leadership®: www.situational.com
- Situational Leadership® II: www.kenblanchard.com

For an effective link between leadership style and the leader's emotional intelligence, covering not just the authoritative and democratic styles, but four others too, try:
- *The New Leaders*, Daniel Goleman, Richard Boyatzis and Annie McKee, Time Warner Paperbacks, 2003

2 ACTION CENTRED LEADERSHIP

QUICK SUMMARY

Our second leadership model is John Adair's Action Centred Leadership. It focuses on the group you are leading and their needs. Your job is to meet them.

- Task need: getting the job done
- Team need: building and maintaining the team
- Individual need: developing the individuals in the team

These three needs overlap. Meeting any one need will have a positive effect on one or both of the others. For example:

- Meeting the individual's needs frees them up to participate fully
- Building a sense of team cohesion helps tasks get done effectively
- A sense of pride in achieving a task gives the team cause to celebrate

Adair argues that there are eight functions you must carry out, to meet these needs. These functions can be learned, practised, observed and refined. When you do this, you will improve your leadership.

QUICK SUMMARY

The three needs that form
your role as a leader

**Achieving
the task**

**Building and
maintaining
the team**

**Developing
the
individual**

The Three Circles diagram is a trademark of John Adair, and is used with his permission.

2 ACTION CENTRED LEADERSHIP

HOW IT WORKS

Task need

As leader, you have brought the group together to achieve the task. They need clarity and a sense of purpose. The group must know what it has to achieve and the reasons why. Crucially, each member must know what you expect of them.

Team need

A group functions best when it is held together by a shared sense of purpose. With good leadership, the group can evolve into a team that collaborates to get things done effectively, efficiently and with a sense of pride in its collective work. To meet this need, create a shared culture for the group by setting and maintaining standards. You must ensure they have the resources they need, encourage a shared sense of responsibility, and help the team to celebrate their successes.

Individual need

People are at the heart of your team. Their individual needs are both physical and psychological. Get to know and value each individual, ensure that their working conditions are fair, and provide them with the recognition, status and opportunities to develop in a way that will build confidence and keep them motivated.

THE EIGHT FUNCTIONS OF LEADERSHIP

To meet the team's three needs, Adair set out eight functions of leadership:

1. **Defining the task** – Set out a clear goal and objectives for your team. Ensure that the scope of their work is bounded appropriately and that they understand the context of what they are doing.

2. **Planning** – Work with your team to put together a plan that breaks the task into stages and lays out clear roles for team members. Be creative, think through options and seek appropriate balances between certainty and flexibility; control and autonomy.

3. **Briefing** – Use your plan to build a shared understanding among your team. Communicate clearly, simply and in vivid terms. Use this as a chance also to listen to and address individuals' questions, concerns and insights.

4. **Controlling** – Get the most from the assets and resources available; not least from your team. Monitor performance and intervene if it is not optimum. Gradually build self-reliance so your team can monitor and control their own work.

THE EIGHT FUNCTIONS OF LEADERSHIP

5. **Evaluating** – Constantly review performance and give timely feedback to the team and individuals against the objectives you set when you defined the task. It will be motivating and improve performance. Remember: give feedback on the good stuff too!

6. **Motivating** – Some ideas: demonstrate your own positive motivation, recognise and celebrate achievement, build relationships, give people responsibility and chances to learn, and create a fair and inspiring environment.

7. **Organising** – Set up systems and processes to help your team work efficiently. Keep your team free to work on the task by taking responsibility for some essential team admin and use your own time well by monitoring the balance of time you give to leading and doing.

8. **Providing an example** – Decide what message you want to give your team – then live it. *'Be the change you want to see in the world'* said Gandhi. This is about setting standards and demonstrating your integrity, so it starts with knowing your own values and ethics.

HOW GOOD IS ACTION CENTRED LEADERSHIP?

Action Centred Leadership gives you a firm agenda for what to do when leading a team, making leadership into a craft that anyone can learn. It continues to be a very successful model taught in a wide range of contexts to new managers and team leaders. It does, however, place the leader's action at the centre of the team's functioning. For many, this is not a satisfactory end-point. It is merely a necessary stage in the development of a self-confident and self-managing team.

The theme of communication is implicit in many of Adair's eight functions. This is an essential part of leadership that may merit a higher profile. Encouraging communication between team members is key to creating a team that will continue to work well when the leader is absent. This resilience is valuable and might be referred to as 'team sustainability'.

A common complaint about Action Centred Leadership is that it is 'obvious'; no more than common sense. This makes it all the more valuable, as common sense is not that common. You will do consistently well when you apply simple models that work. This one does.

2 ACTION CENTRED LEADERSHIP

VARIATIONS ON A THEME
LINKS TO OTHER LEADERSHIP MODELS

As a model of leadership, Action Centred Leadership is complemented by other functional models that address a leader's roles:

- **Transformational Leadership** has four roles: inspirational motivation, consideration for the individual, intellectual stimulation and idealised influence (acting as a role-model). James McGregor Burns inspired this model, and it was further developed by Bernard Bass. Contrast this with **Transactional Leadership** which relies on give-and-take to get things done

- **The Leadership Challenge** by James Kouzes and Barry Posner sets out five challenges: modelling the way, inspiring a shared vision, challenging the process, enabling others to act, and encouraging the heart. These resemble Adair's functions and, indeed, the roles of the transformational leader

- Robert Greenleaf's idea of **Servant Leadership** emphasises the role of a leader as a 'servant' of their team and a steward of its resources. In many ways, Adair's thinking preceded this model, by placing so much emphasis on the leader's role in meeting the needs of their team and the individuals within it

VARIATIONS ON A THEME
LINKS TO OTHER MODELS IN THIS BOOK

As a fundamental management model, Action Centred Leadership links to most models in this book. Four are especially relevant:

- Tuckman's model of **Group Formation** shows how you need to change your style to meet the shifting needs of your team, and also shows how the team can grow beyond Adair's model and become self-managing

- The two models of **Motivation** in this book, McClelland's and Vroom's, will be useful to anybody who wants to get the best from their team members

- Adair also uses Tannenbaum and Schmidt's **Leadership Continuum**. This shows the degrees to which you can find a balance between exerting your own will and preferred solution on your team, and offering freedom for team members to find their own solution

- Boyd's **OODA Loop** brings Adair's planning, controlling, organising, and evaluating functions of leadership into a simple framework

LEARN MORE

John Adair's Action Centred Leadership

- *Effective Leadership 2nd edition*, John Adair, Pan Macmillan, 2009
- *Leadership and Motivation: The Fifty-fifty Rule and the Eight Key Principles of Motivating Others,* John Adair, Kogan Page, 2006
- *Develop your Leadership Skills*, John Adair, Kogan Page/Sunday Times, 2007

For a critical overview:
- *John Adair: Fundamentals of Leadership*, Jonathan Gosling, Peter Case, and Morgen Witzel, Palgrave Macmillan, 2007

Other models of leadership

- *Transformational Leadership*, Bernard M Bass, Lawrence Erlbaum Associates Inc,1982
- *The Leadership Challenge*, James M Kouzes and Barry Z Posner, Jossey Bass, 2008
- *Servant Leadership: A Journey into the Nature of Legitimate Power and Greatness*, Robert K Greenleaf, Paulist Press International, 2002

3 TUCKMAN'S GROUP DEVELOPMENT

INTRODUCTION

Of all of the models of group development, Tuckman's Forming, Storming, Norming, Performing model is, perhaps, the best known. Possibly it is too well-known: many people quote it and many of them do so at second or third hand – so missing some of the subtlety and power of the model.

Why has it been so successful?
Certainly its success is partly down to how good the model is at explaining and predicting behaviours. But other models are good too. Bruce Tuckman himself recognised that this is not always enough. Words matter too, and he did extraordinarily well in finding a set of rhyming labels for the phases he identified, that also capture their essence extremely precisely.

'Quotability may be the key to success.'

Bruce Wayne Tuckman

3 TUCKMAN'S GROUP DEVELOPMENT

THE PROBLEM

Put a group of people into close proximity, and their behaviour will change. This is the basis of many reality TV programmes. The way the group's behaviour changes, and how to secure effective performance from it, are questions faced by many managers.

We find this important because groups illustrate many of the polarities that western culture struggles with: autonomy versus dependence, collaboration versus competition, equality versus hierarchy. It is almost an article of faith for many that a well formed group can be greater than the sum of its parts. So the challenge is, take the people you have and transform them into an effective team.

This is particularly relevant in today's workplace. We have long been used to small work groups. More recently, organisations have devoted increasing resources to short-term project activity, as a way to create change, or a special product or service. The principal challenges are: to understand what is going on within the group, as the dynamics shift; to secure high levels of performance in ever shorter times, and to get the best from each member of the group.

QUICK SUMMARY

In the 1960s, Bruce Tuckman looked at the sequence in which groups develop. By reviewing studies of groups in a range of settings, he created a model of four stages. The terms he coined for the stages have made the model memorable, evoking the characteristics well, and with a pleasing rhyme.

In 1977, Tuckman worked with Mary Ann Jensen to review the model; they added a fifth stage.

QUICK SUMMARY

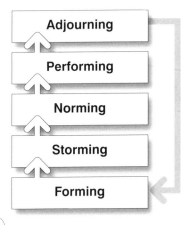

Adjourning Stage – the dissolution of the group and the sense of loss that members feel when they separate.

Performing Stage – the group gains confidence, taking on flexible roles and working together to solve problems and get results.

Norming Stage – the group finds ways to work together and become cohesive. They get on with the task and exchange ideas and information.

Storming Stage – conflict emerges, as group members assert themselves, and react emotionally to the task they are set.

Forming Stage – the group begins here. Members look for ways to interact, are dependent upon the group's leader and try to figure out what is expected of them.

3 TUCKMAN'S GROUP DEVELOPMENT

FORMING

In the first stage, individuals don't know one another, nor what is expected of them. You will see excitement and enthusiasm but also uncertainty and fear. People will appear hesitant and dependent upon whoever is leading. As a group, you will see attempts to learn about each other and test out what behaviours are acceptable, as members seek out rules and boundaries.

The group will often not have a clear idea of the task for which they have been brought together. They will try to define the job and find a way to tackle it. The group needs a goal, clear expectations and some ground rules. As a leader, you must supply these by setting out a clear purpose and objectives, asking for participation. Then allocate tasks and secure commitment to them. Your leadership style needs to be fairly directive at this stage. Also set ground rules and reinforce them with your own behaviour.

Above all, express confidence in the group, so that they feel valued. Allowing people to contribute is the best way to overcome their anxieties and harness their initial enthusiasm. At the end of the norming stage, people are starting to feel part of the group. Now, personalities will start to assert themselves more strongly.

STORMING

Now personal agendas come to the fore. People can become defensive and question decisions, even challenging the leadership. More assertive members will vie for power and control of the group, while the less assertive will seek a safe niche. The group's mood and confidence may dip. You will start to see differing interpretations of the task, that can lead to tension, arguments, jealousy and even outright conflict, as group members compete for influence over each other.

The group may also resist the task, or elements of it. This can be due to growing recognition of its difficulties, or uncertainty about their capacity to tackle it. You may see an emotional response from some, and a desire to take charge in others.

The group needs leadership and, if their leader doesn't give it, someone else will. The team leader may not be the most dominant personality, so will have to dig deep to assert their legitimate leadership. They must clarify and enforce roles, and focus on process, ground rules and supporting the group, taking care of less assertive members. The group needs clear direction and outcomes.

Despite a frequent focus on conflict resolution, storming can be a very creative phase.

3 TUCKMAN'S GROUP DEVELOPMENT

NORMING

In the third stage, resistance to the task diminishes as the group starts to feel a greater sense of cohesion. Criticisms and feedback become constructive and members start to co-operate. You will see agreed standards of behaviour (norms) become accepted and the group often gives a collective sigh of relief that things are working out.

Individuals will feel a pressure to conform to these norms; they give people the confidence to participate, by strengthening clarity of roles and responsibilities. Many are glad to get on with their tasks, as a rest from the highly social and emotional storming stage. This is a very productive time.

The pressure to conform carries the risk of people being subsumed within the group. This can lead to 'Group-think', a term coined by Irving Janis to represent the lack of challenge to ideas and decisions in a group where individuals feel a strong need to conform. A leader can overcome Group-think by encouraging members to value each other's distinctive experience. True co-operation will arise by building networks of working relationships among the group. Above all, the leader must encourage the group's growing confidence by easing off on directive leadership behaviours.

PERFORMING

At last, true collaboration emerges, with the group working together towards a common goal. The structure is flexible and pragmatic, based on mutual respect, trust and liking. Any inter-personal problems are dealt with in a mature way. Individuals are committed to, but not subsumed into, the group. They can express themselves in an atmosphere of real respect. This inter-dependence is characteristic of a team. There is a shared sense of pride in what they are doing.

This focuses the group on its objectives, and you will see enormous energy channelled to achieving the task, with effective problem-solving and decision-making. Leadership must be subtle. Members need little or no guidance; just a light touch of advice and support. An observer would find it hard to spot the leader: instead, they'd see individual acts of leadership as different team members take on the role and then step back.

The leader's job, therefore, is to maintain the environment in which the team can thrive, provide the resources they need, and shield them from distractions.

BEYOND PERFORMING

Adjourning … or _Mourning_ – When a successful group disbands there is a sense of loss, leading some to call this the _mourning_ stage. People need to mark the transition and celebrate their achievements, in preparation for whatever is next. Tuckman and Jensen called this stage 'adjourning', describing it as _'a stage for which a perfect rhyme could not be found'_.

Yawning – Some refer to a point where a team gets bored – no longer feeling stretched by their work, they start to withdraw. Efficiency drops, leading to disaffection and a fragmenting of the group. The leader's role is to re-establish purpose, set new objectives, and stretch the group with meaningful work.

Transforming – When change hits the group – someone leaving, a new recruit, or a new task – the uncertainty can lead to a search for new norms, renewed conflict over roles and influence, or even a need to completely re-orient the group. The leader must be aware that a transformation can throw the team out of its performing state and will need to change leadership style accordingly.

3 TUCKMAN'S GROUP DEVELOPMENT

HOW GOOD IS TUCKMAN'S MODEL?

Tuckman's model is very widely used – doubtless one of the best known models in this book. Has it earned this status? Of the many critiques, four deserve particular attention:

1. How well does it apply?

Tuckman's work very clearly applied to 'small groups' although many would consider the upper end of the size range he studied (30) to be a large group. He looked at groups in training, therapy, laboratory and natural settings, so the evidence base is strong. Perhaps the main critique is that his was secondary research, reviewing and systematising the work of many researchers. Most of the subsequent models of group formation are little more than restatements of his, with different labels.

2. Isn't team effectiveness more complex?

While a four- or five-stage model cannot give you all the criteria for effective group performance, the description of the performing stage does set out the conditions that favour it. However, it is also clear that the group can be effective in other stages when well led and managed: harnessing the enthusiasm of a newly formed team, or the creative energy of a team in the storming stage.

HOW GOOD IS TUCKMAN'S MODEL?

3. Aren't the stages artificial?

Yes, but this is the nature of a model; and competing models choose different boundaries. The model says nothing about the pace with which a group moves through the stages – this depends on the context. The sequence of stages, however, invites more debate. While many will recognise the pattern, it is not universal. Groups can get stuck at one stage, regress, experience two stages at once, or cycle around.

An example is when a group forms quickly to tackle an urgent task with single-minded vigour. With no time to storm, they move quickly from forming to norming and even performing. When the pressure releases and they can operate in a more relaxed way, rivalries and disagreements emerge and come to a head. The group will storm.

4. Has Tuckman dumbed down a complex process?

Simplified, yes. But don't let the catchy terminology fool you. The real problem is not that the model over-simplifies reality; it simplifies to just the right level. The problem is that too many people think they understand all they need to from a cursory inspection of the labels. Understood properly, this model has real predictive, explanatory and developmental power.

LEARN MORE

Group and Team Development

- *Developmental Sequence in Small Groups,* Bruce W Tuckman, Psychological Bulletin, Volume 63, Number 6 (also available to download from the internet), and *Stages of Small-Group Development Revisited*, Bruce W Tuckman and Mary Ann Jensen, Group and Organisation Studies, Volume 2, Number 4
- *Organizational Behaviour: An Introductory Text*, Andrzej Huczynski and David Buchanan, Financial Times/Prentice Hall, 2006
- *The Wisdom of Teams*, Jon R Katzenbach and Douglas K Smith, McGraw-Hill Professional, 2005

More in this pocketbook

- Adair's **Action Centred Leadership** looks at what you need to do to lead a team. Combined with an understanding of Tuckman's model, you can adapt the emphasis of your leadership to move the group quickly through
- The themes that characterise Tuckman's stages (group and task functions) are also the focus of McClelland's theory of **Motivational Needs**, which he describes as affiliation, achievement and power

MOTIVATING PEOPLE AT WORK

4 Expectancy Theory

5 Motivational Needs

THE PROBLEM

WHAT GOVERNS OUR CHOICES

How do people make decisions about what they will and won't do, and how much effort to put in? This is an essential question for any manager who wants to get the maximum amount of work from their people. And, if you are a manager who prefers carrots to sticks, you will want this to arise from a positive commitment.

Of course, you would think that there is one way that is guaranteed to get someone motivated to do something: ask them to do something they already want to do. In fact, even this is not guaranteed to work, when, for example, there is a conflict with duty or an alternative option.

The problem of motivation boils down to two questions:
- **Arousal:** What gets us interested in doing something?
- **Choice:** What makes us decide whether to pursue it?

The next two models deal with each of these questions in turn; choice first, with Expectancy Theory; then arousal, with Motivational Needs.

QUICK SUMMARY

Victor Vroom described his Expectancy Theory of motivation in terms of a mathematical equation – a choice he later regretted. It is much easier to understand as a story.

I want my car washed and, luckily, I have four children. I ask my older son if he will do it, but he says, *'No. Whenever I wash your car, you always criticise and say it's not clean enough'*. Vroom called the link between the effort we put in and the performance we believe we can achieve, **Expectancy**.

So I ask my older daughter. She knows that she can clean my car well, so I promise a small gift. But she says *'no'* too. *'Whenever you promise me a gift, you always forget.'* Vroom called the link between performance and anticipated outcome, **Instrumentality**.

QUICK SUMMARY

I next ask my younger son to clean the car. He knows he always does a good job and I have never let him down with a present. But he declines, saying, *'There is nothing I want at the moment; I'd rather go and play with my friends'*. Vroom called the value we associate with a reward, the **Valence**.

My younger daughter has no such concerns. She knows she can do a great job, trusts I'll honour my promise, and also wants a new DVD. For her, the desire to achieve the reward, and the confidence that she can earn it, make the effort worthwhile.

QUICK SUMMARY

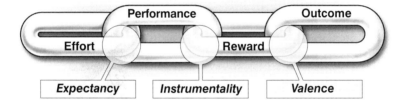

Performance

Outcome

Effort **Reward**

Expectancy *Instrumentality* *Valence*

Expectancy theory is like the links of a chain. The strength of the link between the effort you put in and the results you get is called *expectancy*. The link between your performance and the reward you are promised is called *instrumentality*. The strength of the link between the promised reward and the value to you of the outcome you associate with it is called *valence*.

EXPECTANCY: EFFORT & RESULTS

If I ask you to do something, and you put in the effort, how confident are you that you will get the results I expect? Your answer to this is what Vroom termed *expectancy*. Expectancy is therefore a subjective measure – it is not a reflection of your actual capability, but of your beliefs about your ability to get the result I want. The more you believe something can be done, the more you are likely to want to do it. Expectancy can range from:

Zero – *'I believe it is impossible'*   to   **One** – *'I am sure I can do it'*

In the next section on Motivational Needs, you will see how McClelland found that certain people will be demotivated by a task that is too easy; people with a high *'need for achievement'* are most motivated when the expectancy is about half.

Here are some things you can do to increase expectancy at work:
- Provide appropriate support, encouragement and ongoing review
- Give a thorough briefing with context, key steps and advice
- Ensure access to the right resources, equipment and materials

4 EXPECTANCY THEORY

INSTRUMENTALITY: PERFORMANCE & REWARD

Instrumentality is a subjective judgement by the person you want to motivate. It measures the extent to which they believe that, if they deliver the results you require, you will deliver the reward you promised. Clearly, nobody will work for a promised reward if they doubt it will materialise. Yet many organisations – and managers too – will happily break a promise in the belief that people will forget and be fooled next time.
Instrumentality can range from:

Zero – *'I don't believe you'*   **to**   **One –** *'I am sure you'll deliver it'*

The reward can be one provided by the organisation: a promotion, a commendation, a bonus, or even a pat on the back. These are *extrinsic* rewards; beyond our direct control. We can equally be motivated by an *intrinsic* reward; something we ourselves want, like the fulfilment of a personal need or desire.

To boost instrumentality at work:
- Make your promises plausible
- Create a track record of keeping your promises
- Distance yourself from others who break their promises

'Fool me once, shame on you.
Fool me twice, shame on me.'
Anon

(49)

4 EXPECTANCY THEORY

VALENCE: REWARD & PERSONAL OUTCOME

Valence is where this model links directly to other models of motivation that talk about *what* motivates us. It measures the value we attach to the reward we are promised and how that reward links to outcomes or goals in our lives. The greater the attraction of the reward, the higher its valence, which can range from:

Minus one – *'I really don't want it'* **to**

Zero – *'I don't care about it'* **to**

Plus one – *'I really do want it'.*

We are not only motivated by the value we attach to the reward. Some work is intrinsically motivating – just achieving the results is reward enough. As an example, few get rich writing a book, yet many take on the challenge and feel a huge sense of achievement that justifies the effort. So valence can also link to an intrinsic reward.

To boost valence at work:
- Find out what your colleagues want, enjoy, and value in life
- Understand how other models, which describe what motivates us, apply
- Provide work that is intrinsically motivating – provides its own rewards

4 EXPECTANCY THEORY

VROOM'S EXPECTANCY THEORY EQUATION

Vroom originally articulated his model as a mathematical equation. He later felt that this introduced a bogus sense that the model could be tested empirically. What the equation does, however, is show how the three terms interact.

Motivation = Expectancy × Instrumentality × Valence

The multiplication means that if any single component is very small, then your motivation to act will be low. To be highly motivated, each term must be near to one. And because valence can be negative – the outcome is an unwanted one – so can motivation. In this case, you would be motivated to avoid the action concerned.

There may be multiple outcomes from an action. So Vroom suggested we would have to add up the individual motivations to get the total motivation.

Total motivation = Motivation 1 + Motivation 2 + Motivation 3 +

VARIATIONS ON A THEME
LINKS TO OTHER MODELS

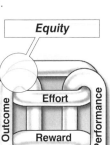

Expectancy theory is central to ideas of motivation in the workplace. Just as Vroom developed his thinking from earlier models, others have sought to complement or improve on his simple model. Two strands are worth unpicking.

- **Needs Theories: Maslow, Hertzberg, Alderfer, McClelland and others**. There are many models of what motivates us or, in Vroom's terms, what has a high valence. These motivators are our needs, wants, desires – even lusts! We look at McClelland's model in detail in the next section

- **Adams' Equity Theory**. Stacy Adams argued that we are motivated by a need for fairness, and will work hard to reduce inequity. Often we view the valence of a reward not simply in its own terms, but against our perception of how others around us are rewarded for a similar effort

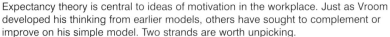

HOW GOOD IS EXPECTANCY THEORY?

Vroom did not set out to create a complete model of motivation. If he were to start again, he says, he would pay more attention to what causes us to start or stop our behaviour. Other criticisms are more substantial.

The model assumes behaviour is rational and calculating: it rarely is. We often make decisions based on simple, almost reflexive, behaviours, called heuristics. If you are trying to gauge my motivation, you must gauge *my* perceptions of expectancy and instrumentality, rather than yours, even if you have better knowledge. This introduces bias and prejudice.

Expectancy Theory ignores wholly the nature of the work. This surely influences our motivation – we don't like all work equally. Finally, this model assumes that explicit rewards are valued. There is evidence that explicit rewards actually diminish our implicit sense of satisfaction in a job well done, by making the reward our objective, rather than the result. Think of the pleasure of reading a novel for itself versus reading a set text for an exam. Having said all of this, Expectancy Theory makes sense. Understanding it can prevent you from sabotaging motivation.

5 MOTIVATIONAL NEEDS

QUICK SUMMARY

David McClelland looked at the motivations that made nations and individuals successful. He focused on three motivational needs. These help to explain why some people are successful in their work roles and others are not. They also allow you to identify which roles will best suit you or your team members. We each have all three of these needs; it is their relative strengths that influence how we perform in a role.

'Almost all theories of motivation make some assumptions about individual needs, or drives.'

Charles Handy

The need for achievement
This is a drive to succeed and excel. People with a high need to achieve are competitive, like solving problems, and readily take personal responsibility.

The need for power
This is a drive to influence others. People with a high need for power like to take charge and seek prestige, either for themselves or for their organisation.

The need for affiliation
This is a drive for sociability. People with a high need for affiliation like co-operation and friendly relationships, and dislike competition and discord.

QUICK SUMMARY

McClelland identified three overlapping needs that are important in understanding our motivation to succeed.

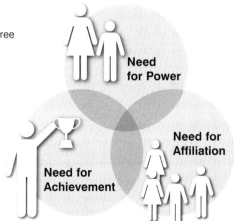

Need for Power

Need for Affiliation

Need for Achievement

THE NEED FOR ACHIEVEMENT

McClelland initially focused on people with a high need for achievement, who are motivated by achieving goals and meeting standards – whether their own or ones imposed on them. They get a buzz out of solving problems and seek mechanisms to get direct feedback on their performance. Salespeople are a typical example.

They may be risk takers, but their risks are calculated. In Vroom's terms, they favour tasks with an expectancy – a likelihood of success – of around 50%. If the chance of success is too high, there is no sense of achievement if they do succeed. They also avoid opportunities with too little chance of success. Entrepreneurs are an example.

People with a high need for achievement do not necessarily make good managers; they can be too focused on their own success, rather than that of others. When they are in a leadership role, it is often a pace-setting *'do as I do'* style that they adopt.

To motivate people with a high need for achievement:
- Set them challenges, problems to solve, or processes to improve
- Give them access to performance data so they can see how they are doing
- Put them in competition with others, or set up targets for them to meet

THE NEED FOR POWER

McClelland concluded that the need for power is vital for managers in organisational settings. People with a high need for power try to influence others. It is not about (naked) authoritarianism, though it can become so. They do, however, like to be in charge and enjoy the associated prestige. McClelland distinguished two forms of power:

- Managers with a need for **institutional power** wield their power with care. They tend to be controlled in their use of power and use it to benefit their organisation
- Managers who need **personal power** are less inhibited and more impulsive, wielding power more for their own purposes. They can be directive, controlling, rude, or worse. Unsurprisingly, McClelland found them less effective

The most successful also have a significant drive either to achieve (giving a sense of purpose) or to be affiliative (leading them to use their interpersonal skills).

To motivate people with a high need for power:

- Allow them to form their own judgement and put their case
- Recognise and publicise their achievements
- Offer them opportunities to lead or to represent your organisation

THE NEED FOR AFFILIATION

The need for affiliation is less likely to dominate in highly successful people. The focus on co-operation and harmony is a powerful adjunct to another dominant need, but alone does not provide enough motivational force for what we commonly perceive as success.

Perhaps the strongest demonstration of our common need for affiliation is the *Hawthorne Effect*. Elton Mayo was studying the impact of improved lighting on workers' motivation and productivity at the Hawthorne Plant in Chicago. One group got better lighting, the other didn't. Both groups increased productivity. Confused, Mayo reduced lighting for both groups: productivity increased. Researchers concluded that because they all knew they were part of the study, it was the extra attention that motivated them.

To motivate people with a high need for affiliation:
- Offer opportunities to work in teams and in roles where pleasing others is valued
- Establish strong group norms that they can subscribe to and encourage them to organise the team socially
- Give plenty of positive support and attention; seek people's opinions

EXTREMES OF THE THREE NEEDS

We have seen how you can recognise high needs. What behaviours will you see in people with low needs, or where extreme needs leave them fearful of loss?

The need for achievement
People with a low need for achievement avoid responsibility and can come across as apathetic. Some are fearful and, rather than being motivated to achieve, work hard to avoid failure, becoming over-cautious and unwilling to make commitments.

The need for power
People with a low need for power tend to be submissive and dependent on others. Those who fear losing power can make shows of strength, abuse their power while they have it, and be obsequious towards those they believe have power over them.

The need for affiliation
People with a low need for affiliation tend to be aloof, perhaps even afraid of social contact. Those fearful of losing affiliation show a strong need to please and often say *'yes'* to any request rather than risk conflict. They make promises they cannot keep and buy affection with favours that ultimately harm or demean themselves.

VARIATIONS ON A THEME

LINKS TO OTHER MODELS

McClelland's is one of many models that focus on needs. The last two mentioned are also in this pocketbook.

- Maslow's **Hierarchy of Needs** is well known, but is not based on research and has little predictive power. It feels right but has little practical advice to offer

- Alderfer's **ERG Model** is a development from Maslow; simpler and less prescriptive. It suggests we balance our needs for Existence, Relatedness (to others), and Growth

- **Drivers** in Transactional Analysis are behaviours we consistently display and therefore motivate our work style (or sabotage it). They are to: Please Others, Be Strong, Try Hard, Be Perfect, and Hurry Up

- French and Raven's **Power Bases** give a structure for understanding how individuals meet their need for organisational or personal power. Connection Power will appeal to those with a high need for affiliation while those with a high need to achieve will value Expert Power, not for the power, but for the expertise

- **The Leadership Continuum** offers a range of leadership behaviours. Among the forces that will influence your choice of style will be your dominant need

HOW GOOD ARE MOTIVATIONAL NEEDS?

McClelland and his collaborators have done a lot of work comparing the strengths of people's needs with their success in their work roles. There are clear relationships between need for achievement and productivity, and need for power and managerial success. One criticism is that there is less research on the need for affiliation. This model also predicts job satisfaction reasonably well, based on the alignment or misalignment between a person's dominant needs and their job role.

Unlike some models of motivation, these three needs seem to apply across cultures. McClelland does not say who will have which needs and how they will balance. Instead, we acquire them through the totality of our life experiences. There are differences from culture to culture in which needs dominate, and the extent to which they impact upon success. In the west, there are also clear male-female differences.

What about other needs? Henry Murray identified 27 human needs and others have offered more. A full understanding of human motivation surely must account for all of these needs, which is why other models, like Maslow's, remain popular.

5 MOTIVATIONAL NEEDS

LEARN MORE

Motivation in general

A wide range of popular management books and texts on organisational behaviour discuss motivation in general and Vroom's and McClelland's models in particular. Or, for a pocketful of tools and techniques, we recommend:

- *The Motivation Pocketbook,* Max A Eggert, Management Pocketbooks, 1999

Expectancy theory

- *Work and Motivation,* Victor H Vroom, Jossey Bass, 1994

- *On the Origins of Expectancy Theory* in the book *Great Minds in Management,* Ken G Smith and Michael A Hitt, OUP Oxford, 2007

Motivational needs

Two key stages of McClelland's thinking are represented in Harvard Business Review articles, available as reprints:

- *Business Drive and National Achievement,*
  David C McClelland, Harvard Business Review, July-August 1962

- *Power is the Great Motivator,*
  David C McClelland, Harvard Business Review, HBR Classic, January-February 1995

UNDERSTANDING PEOPLE AT WORK

UNDERSTANDING PEOPLE AT WORK

INTRODUCTION

Three models will help you to understand people's behaviour in the workplace:

The NLP Model of Communication will help you to improve how you communicate with colleagues and partners, both sending and receiving ideas, by providing a model for how to communicate effectively and understanding what can go wrong.

Power Bases will help you to see where power lies in your organisation.

But, first of all:

Transactional Analysis, with its roots in therapy, is an enormous and rich subject – more a cluster of models than a single model. Its focus is on the interactions, or 'transactions' between people.

6 TRANSACTIONAL ANALYSIS

THE PROBLEM

Communication at work can go wrong in so
many ways. The day to day problems of
communicating clearly and getting on with one
another are exacerbated by differences in the
workplace, due to factors like personality,
seniority, experience, and expertise.

'Why is he always
so critical of me?'

'Why is she always
so defensive?'

Communication problems are rarely one-off events. More often, they are part of a pattern
of behaviour that can become ingrained into the relationship between two co-workers,
between a manager and staff member, or a supplier and client. Ultimately, these patterns
can disrupt effective communication, reduce efficient working, and leave one or both parties
feeling frustrated, unhappy, or even exhausted.

A model that helps you to understand why people interact as they do will be immensely
useful. It will also help to be able to explain your own interactions. Perhaps most useful
would be a model that helps you to change disruptive patterns and put your communication
with certain colleagues onto an effective footing. Let's look at some examples.

THE PROBLEM

NOT FEELING COMFORTABLE

There are many management situations where we feel uncomfortable communicating what we know is the right message. The conversation could be awkward, so we start to fear it. Our fear becomes visible to the other person and, subconsciously, they react to it. The dialogue does not go well, and this reinforces the pattern for next time. How many of these examples are familiar to you?

- Agreeing performance targets
- Allocating or delegating work to certain team members
- Giving feedback on under-performance

THE PROBLEM

PLAYING GAMES

Sometimes it feels like someone's pattern of behaviour has become a habit. Worse than that, we can feel like they know what they are doing and are almost manipulating the situation.

We can then feel bad and not know how to break the cycle:

- *'Now look what you've done – if it weren't for you …'*
- *'Oh poor me, it's not my fault …'*
- *'Aha, I've caught you, now I'll make you pay …'*

QUICK SUMMARY

Eric Berne developed Transactional Analysis (TA) to help understand how we communicate, and to put his ideas into a simple language. At the core of his model are three Ego States, or ways of behaving. We each move among all three, but when we initiate or receive a message, we exhibit one of these three states:

- **Parent state:** Behaving in ways we derive from what we have learned from others in the past, as we feel we are *supposed to*
- **Adult state:** Behaving in ways that are appropriate to the present, governed by awareness and reason
- **Child state:** Behaving in ways that we think worked for us in the past, with a focus on our own immediate needs and desires

When we interact with another person, our communications consist of transactions from one of our Ego States to one of the other person's. It is the nature of these transactions that will help you to understand what is going on and make choices about how to handle future transactions. Clearly, in the workplace, **Adult-Adult** transactions will most often give you the results you want to create. An uneven relationship can, however, frustrate this desire.

QUICK SUMMARY

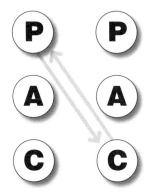

The first person to speak initiates a transaction from the Parent ego state. This gets a response from the receiver's Child ego state. For example:

Stimulus: 'This report is not good enough. You'll have to re-write it.' (Critical Parent)
Response: 'I'm really sorry. Please help me to get it right.'(Adapted Child)

THE EGO STATES

The ego states describe how we function in the world. We each have helpful behaviours that we do well and other less helpful behaviours that, when not feeling at our best, we find ourselves sliding into. Ego states are neither good nor bad. Each can play a role in healthy behaviours and each can act as a barrier to helpful communication. With awareness, we can start to make appropriate choices.

The Adult will assess everything calmly and rationally. In this state, we listen hard, try to understand, and apply its knowledge and experience. We also reassess a situation in the light of new evidence. The Adult state can appear cold and unemotional, but can also seem grounded and aware of their true situation.

THE EGO STATES

There are two ways we can express the Parent state and each can have positive or negative aspects to our behaviour.

The Critical Parent tells you what to do, can be judgemental, prejudiced and over-bearing. In this state, we rarely take responsibility, preferring to find fault or to blame 'circumstances'. We like to conform and follow standards, which can either create blind obedience or, on the positive side, create structure, organisation and security. In the Critical Parent state, we feel willing to tell others what to do.

The Nurturing Parent is caring, shows concern for our welfare, allowing us to explore, while trying to help. In this state, we can also be over-indulgent, patronising, even smothering at times. We want others to do well and can be tempted to give too much of ourselves. This state can bring out our compassionate nature and allows us to understand and accept other people's feelings.

THE EGO STATES

Like the Parent state, there are two ways we can express the Child state; again, each with positive or negative aspects to our behaviour.

The Free Child is the state where we can express our emotions without restraint, letting our needs and desires be known. In this state, we can be selfish and will try to do what we want – often heedless of risks or cautions. We can also be aggressive, wilful and competitive. This state is the fun-loving source of our creativity, spontaneity, innovation, and our 'joie de vivre'. The positive and negative behaviours might be described as immature.

The Adapted Child is anxious to please. In this state, our primary drive is obedience and a strong need to fit in, so we are keen to be friendly, to co-operate, to learn and do well. This is how we strive to improve. We can also exhibit nervous and submissive behaviours, linked to feelings of inferiority. These same feelings can also give rise to rebellious behaviours, as the adapted child tries to demonstrate its independence.

TRANSACTIONS

Complementary transactions – Communication flows when the response comes from the ego state addressed by the stimulus, and is aimed at the ego state that initiated the stimulus. Good flow is not enough: at work, a Parent-Child interaction can feel awful for one or both. A Child-Child transaction can be fun – *'let's play'* – but inappropriate. A Parent-Parent transaction may build rapport – *'Isn't it awful?'* *'Oh, I know'* – but perpetuate prejudice and frustrate progress. Adult-Adult transactions get the job done.

Crossed transactions – When we respond from an ego state not addressed by the stimulus, the transactions will cross and communication breaks down. When this pattern gets locked in, we can get into game-playing. When I address you from Adult to Adult, and you reply *'Who are you to tell me what to do?'* from your Parent to my Child, we have a power struggle.

Hidden, or ulterior, transactions – The overt, or social, transaction may be Adult-Adult: *'This is what I want you to do.'* *'OK, I'll do it.'* But if the real, underlying, transaction is sarcastic, flirtatious or snide, the transaction is hidden. *'I'm sorry to ask you'* (psychologically, Child to Parent) may beget *'OK, but you'll have to pay'* (psychologically, Parent to Child).

GAMES

Games are patterns that involve hidden transactions. What goes on at the psychological level is not what a written transcript would show. Once established we tend to repeat the game. Damage arises because:

- Transactions can become crossed and communication breaks down

- Games invite one 'player' into a subordinate position – or both at different times

- They reinforce limiting perceptions of ourselves and others

Game: 'if it weren't for you ...'
Player A blames Player B for holding them back. When B challenges this (crossed transaction), A takes offence and plays the victim.

Game: 'poor me ...'
Player A feels disadvantaged by someone or something else. A seeks sympathy from B, who gives it in return for gratitude. This feeds A's sense of impotence, diminishing their sense of responsibility for their own situation.

Game: 'now I've got you ...'
On the face of it, Player A simply spots Player B's mistake and points it out. At the psychological level, A has finally caught B out and wants to punish B, shifting blame away from A's own behaviour.

THE DRAMA TRIANGLE

The Drama Triangle is a model developed by Stephen Karpman. In a short article, he analysed three familiar fairy tales, and identified the three roles we need to analyse the emotional structure of a game, or the more complex interactions that he called dramas:

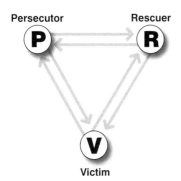

Persecutor: plays an attacking role – often to avoid their own issues

Victim: discounts their own ability to help themselves

Rescuer: takes care of other, and thus disempowers them by denying the Victim's ability to help themselves

THE DRAMA TRIANGLE & GAME

Games start with two or more people, each occupying a corner of the triangle. Players compete to switch position, from victim to persecutor, or from persecutor to rescuer, for example. Players are all in Parent or Child state regardless of which role they take.

Game playing is seductive because there is a pay-off; we either shed responsibility or feel good about our superiority. To avoid games, stay in your Adult ego state. Stay alert to what is going on and don't get drawn in; if you do find yourself in a game, declaring *'this feels familiar'* is the best way to break the cycle and return to Adult state.

USING TRANSACTIONAL ANALYSIS

Scenario 1: Newly appointed manager

If you are a new supervisor, team leader or manager, you probably got the job by being the best candidate: you were not necessarily the oldest, most experienced or longest serving. Managing former colleagues can be uncomfortable; especially if they are older or have more experience.

You may then move into Child state, which you betray with your body language and tone of voice. Become aware of these feelings and recognise your right to manage your team. Make a conscious effort to stay in Adult state. And if colleagues talk to you from their Parent state, avoid getting caught up in their game; stay in Adult state.

USING TRANSACTIONAL ANALYSIS

Scenario 2: Delegation

When you delegate work, you make a conscious decision to ask the most appropriate person to take on the task. Clearly, an Adult-Adult transaction is appropriate. We often find delegation uncomfortable because it feels a bit like we are telling the other person what to do: Parent-Child.

Adult state uses a sound process and is motivated by positive intent. Explain clearly what you want and why, addressing your colleague's Adult state.

Scenario 3: One excuse after another

Here your staff member sees themselves as the victim of your repeated requests – all of which are, to them, unreasonable. You become their persecutor. It serves their need to justify their poor performance, rather than take responsibility for it.

When you have had enough, they may just switch roles and become your rescuer: *'OK, I'll help you out this time'.* Who feels the victim now? Put a stop to it by naming this game and refusing to play.

USING TRANSACTIONAL ANALYSIS

Scenario 4: Recruitment interviews

Game playing can be rife in job interviews – by both parties.

When you are the **interviewer**, stay in Adult state and keep your Critical Parent at bay, pacify the interviewee's scared Child and give it a chance to speak, avoid becoming a rescuer, and decline any opportunities to play games.

When you are the **interviewee**, stay in Adult state and avoid playing the Victim role. Don't play any games of your own (like *'poor me', or 'if it weren't for …'*), and don't get seduced into any games by your interviewer.

HOW GOOD IS TRANSACTIONAL ANALYSIS?

TA has both benefited and suffered from Berne's deliberate use of everyday-sounding terms like Parent, Adult, Child, and Game. This resulted in a wide number of lay people learning and understanding the ideas – exactly what he wanted. It also resulted in two unwanted effects. First, the terms Berne used have specific meanings within TA. Poorly communicated, TA can give rise to errors in understanding and over-simplification. Secondly, some psychology professionals (Berne's own profession) have rather looked down on it for its popularity and seeming simplicity.

There is a great deal more to TA than this short summary, or even a popular TA book, can cover. It has applications as a theory of personality, child development, and psychopathology. Managers, however, can use it to analyse communication and workplace dynamics.

For this purpose, TA is excellent and will repay further study. In essence, it provides intellectual support and an analytical framework for this author's frequent assertion that if you want to understand any workplace interaction, ask yourself: *'what would be going on if this were happening in the playground?'*

6 TRANSACTIONAL ANALYSIS

LEARN MORE

Transactional Analysis

- *TA Today: A New Introduction to Transactional Analysis*, Ian Stewart and Vann Joines, Lifespace Publishing, 1987
- *I'm OK – You're OK*, Thomas Harris, Harper Paperbacks, 2004

A number of training providers are qualified to offer TA training at different levels.

Workplace dynamics

Two other models in this book are enhanced by an understanding of Transactional Analysis, and will supplement your ability to work within an organisation.

- The **NLP Model of Communication** will give you an effective prescription for how to conduct Adult-Adult transactions and will also show why we sometimes misinterpret other people's meanings
- **Power Bases** will look at the different types of power people have within organisations. Differences in power often lead to game playing

INTRODUCTION

When we interpret the information we receive from the world, we make our own version of it, which is not the same as the reality. This is especially true when we communicate with each other. Each of us interprets the other in the context of our own beliefs, prejudices, values, experiences and opinions.

Only when *'what I think you said'* is sufficiently close to *'what you meant to say'* is communication truly effective. The NLP model of communication will help you to understand why and to improve the way you communicate.

'The map is not the territory.'
Alfred Korzybski

THE PROBLEM

'I don't hear what you meant to say: I hear what I think you said.'

Sometimes it seems a wonder that we ever communicate anything. It is not so much that I don't understand you, as I understand you perfectly well. But what I understand and what you meant me to understand are often rather different. And, of course, you don't always understand me, either.

The problems of communication are compounded in times of stress. As a manager, these are likely to be frequent, and they are critical times to ensure you get your message across quickly and accurately. So too are times when a complete understanding of what is said or done is necessary, such as:

- **Difficult messages** when you are giving performance feedback
- **Problem-solving** requires an accurate comprehension of the issue at hand
- **Complex instructions** place a premium on clear explanation
- **Conflict** raises the emotional level, making it harder to understand
- **Times of change** require more and clearer communication

7 NLP MODEL OF COMMUNICATION

THE PROBLEM

We can split the problem of communication into two components.

How we receive information – All sorts of processes, like the limitations of our senses and the prejudices our experiences impose on us, can interfere with our ability to understand what we hear, see and read. We respond to our interpretation, rather than to reality, and the more things we allow to 'get in the way', the poorer our response is.

How we send information – Day to day communication feels so easy to us that we forget what a marvel it is. So we become careless about how our words or actions will be received. When the message we want to convey is more complex, or the situation trickier, our carelessness results in misunderstanding. But who do I blame for you not understanding me? I blame you, because I am perfectly clear what I meant to say!

This is compounded when we are not totally comfortable with what we are saying. Our tone of voice and body language can leak their own messages which conflict with what we are saying. Other people will pick up these mixed messages.

7 NLP MODEL OF COMMUNICATION

QUICK SUMMARY

The NLP Model of Communication stems from the work of John Grinder and Richard Bandler, who collated a body of knowledge about effective communication, which they called Neuro Linguistic Programming, or NLP. Their model suggests that our senses and brains filter the information we receive from the outside world. This can result in our perception being different from reality. They described three filter processes:

- Deletion: removing information that we consider irrelevant
- Distortion: changing our interpretation of the world to fit our own understanding
- Generalisation: taking limited experience and applying it to other situations

These three processes normally serve us well. When applied at the wrong time, to the wrong information, however, they lead us into mistakes.

'The meaning of your communication is the response you get.' Grinder and Bandler also argue that, to get the best results, it will help you to assume this: if someone doesn't understand what you say, or their actions are not what you intended, the problem lies with your communication; not with their understanding. This attitude will help you take responsibility for how you communicate.

QUICK SUMMARY

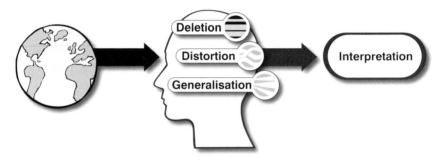

Filters in our brains delete, distort and generalise information we receive, to create the interpretation on which we base our actions.

THE THREE FILTERS

We delete information to prevent overwhelming our brains with the vast amount of sensory data reaching us every second. It is an essential protection mechanism. Sometimes, we delete valuable information. When making decisions we often fall into the 'confirming evidence trap'. This leads us to see evidence that confirms our initial belief and blinds us to data that contradicts our belief.

Distortion

Every time we interpret an external event, we fit it into a framework of pre-existing knowledge. We look for cause and effect, and meaning. Sometimes our analysis is wrong and we find the wrong interpretation. We can also deliberately choose a random or contrary interpretation of information. This is how we innovate and create new ideas.

THE THREE FILTERS

Generalisation

When you visit a new building, how do you know how the doors work? You don't. Instead, you make a generalisation from your experience. This rarely lets you down. But when the generalisation is based on too little evidence, or a limited set of information, it leads us to faulty generalisations that we often refer to as prejudice.

Deletion

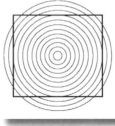

Distortion

Generalisation

THE MEANING OF YOUR COMMUNICATION IS THE RESPONSE YOU GET

If you want to take responsibility for your own communication with others, NLP offers a simple four-step process.

1. Decide on your outcome: what do you want the other person to do or think?
2. Communicate: put out your ideas as effectively as you can.
3. Notice how they respond: do they get it? What are they doing in response?
4. Be flexible: if you didn't get the response you wanted, try a different approach.

Outcome

Communicate

Feedback

Try again

RAPPORT
PEOPLE LIKE PEOPLE LIKE THEMSELVES

Communication builds on rapport. You get rapport with another person when you find common ground. This is why we start conversations with someone we have just met by asking simple questions; we hope to find something in common: *'oh, me too!'* Rapport goes deeper than just common experience; it is often about ideas in common, or values and beliefs. You can also build rapport by being like the other person in more superficial ways: think how you feel when you meet someone with the same name as yours. Notice how groups of friends or work teams conform to similar patterns of dress. Simply following gestures and nodding at appropriate times also helps.

Your gestures and tone of voice also tell us a lot about you. Where they reinforce what you are saying, they tell us that we can believe you. This is called congruence. But if your gestures or voice suggest uncertainty (incongruence), we will almost certainly doubt what you are saying.

When you communicate with someone, notice how they respond. Their expressions, movements and tone of voice will tell you more about how effective your communication is than just their words.

7 NLP MODEL OF COMMUNICATION

WHAT IS NLP?

There are many definitions of NLP, which betrays how hard it can be to pin it down. Cutting through the jargon, it is a body of knowledge and tools about communication. The principal ideas behind NLP are:

- How we use language affects how we think, and vice versa. Practitioners therefore use NLP to influence and also to evaluate other people's concerns
- If you copy what experts do, you will get the same results they do. The process of observing, documenting and reproducing effective behaviour is called 'modelling'

NLP is used in many contexts, from the workplace and personal development, to therapeutic change. The developers of its methods have systematically studied great communicators and therapists to understand what they do and how they do it. From this, NLP has grown into a huge basket of techniques.

For managers, valuable NLP resources are: understanding how to use language effectively; understanding how to manage your state of mind, your confidence, and how you present yourself; and gaining insights into how others think and are motivated.

HOW GOOD IS NLP?

NLP evokes *'love it'* and *'hate it'* reactions and its popularity goes through peaks and troughs. Three factors are perhaps responsible for the extreme views:

1. NLP is presented with a lot of complex jargon. Indeed, the name Neuro Linguistic Programming suggests a level of mind-control which can intimidate or seduce.

2. Some practitioners make extravagant claims for what NLP can achieve.

3. There is a limited research base. A lot of the evidence for the efficacy of NLP techniques is anecdotal.

HOW GOOD IS NLP?

On the other hand, there are also three good reasons to learn more about NLP:

1.   Many people find that much of it really does work. The ideas are taken from observations of effective behaviour. You can apply the modelling process to find out how to replicate the results of your best performers.

2.   NLP is respectful of our potential. It encourages personal responsibility and asserts that we can all access the resources we need to make the changes we want.

3.   The criticism that much of NLP is 'just common sense' can also be seen as a strength. By codifying common sense, we make it more accessible.

You can find much in NLP that is of value to you; and much that is not. If you are prepared to be selective and evaluate each tool on its merits, NLP is a powerful resource.

LEARN MORE

Neuro Linguistic Programming

- *NLP at Work: The Difference that Makes a Difference in Business*, Sue Knight, Nicholas Brealey Publishing Ltd, 2002
- *NLP: Workbook: A Practical Guide to Achieving the Results You Want*, Joseph O'Connor, Thorsons, 2001

Many training providers offer NLP training at different levels, from taster sessions to full Practitioner and Master Practitioner qualifications.

Workplace dynamics

NLP can be read into much of organisational behaviour. Three of the models in this book resonate with core ideas in NLP:

- Like NLP, **Transactional Analysis** stems from a therapeutic approach. You can interpret the Ego State of the listener as influencing how NLP's three filters work
- Vroom's **Expectancy Theory** looks very much like what NLP would describe as a 'strategy' for deciding whether or not to be motivated
- Boyd's **OODA Loop** is very similar to NLP's prescription for effective communication – as indeed is any variant on the plan-do-review cycle

8 POWER BASES

INTRODUCTION

Does it sometimes feel like working life would be easier if it weren't for other people? At one time or another, most of us have found ourselves doing what other people want us to do; not what we want to do. The reason is simple: power.

Power bases are the sources of power and the term was introduced in 1959, by psychologists John R P French and Bertram Raven.

'Life is a search after power...'
Ralph Waldo Emerson

THE PROBLEM

Power is the ability to get others to do what you want, regardless of what they want. As a manager, you will have power over many of the people around you, and others will have power over you. What often surprises us is that some people seem to have power over us, when we don't expect them to.

If you want to get things done in the workplace, you need to be able to navigate your way through the various power bases that your colleagues, clients, suppliers, competitors and business partners have.

- Can you get the things done that you need to?
- Can you get others to do what you need them to?
- Can you work around frustrating blockages?
- Can you avoid being at the beck and call of others?

8 POWER BASES

THE PROBLEM

'How do organisations elicit compliance from their members?' Amitai Etzioni addressed this question, concluding that there are three types of organisation, each wielding a different sort of power.

Coercive Power: Organisations that can enforce compliance by the use of physical force or restraint. Coercive organisations leave members alienated from them. Examples include custodial institutions.

Utilitarian Power: Organisations that achieve compliance by the giving and withholding of rewards. Also called 'remunerative' or 'calculative' organisations; members are committed to the rewards, asking 'what's in it for me?' Businesses tend to be utilitarian.

Normative Power: Organisations that win compliance through conviction to shared beliefs or values. Such organisations create commitment from members who believe the organisation has the right to expect compliance. Voluntary organisations and religions are examples, but many businesses try to create this by appealing to common values.

This model does not tell us how individuals within the organisations secure compliance.

8 POWER BASES

QUICK SUMMARY

John French and Bertram Raven described the sources of power that people have, listing five categories that they called 'social power bases'. The word 'social' implies that the power exists because of the relationship between the holder and the person who is dependent on the holder. This is contrary to other views that power is a part of the organisation (as Etzioni implied) or of individuals themselves.

The first five types are derived from the resources the holder has at their disposal:
1. **Legitimate Power** – based on seniority of position.
2. **Reward Power** – based on ability to offer inducements.
3. **Coercive Power** – based on ability to impose sanctions.
4. **Expert Power** – based on skills and expertise.
5. **Referent Power** – based on personal characteristics; charisma.

Subsequently, they added a further two:
6. **Information Power** – based on the knowledge you can access.
7. **Connection Power** – based on the people you can access.

QUICK SUMMARY

We can divide the powers into two groups: positional power that flows from our status, and personal power, which we earn for ourselves.

French and Raven's original five power bases have been added to – by themselves and by other authors. The most useful addition is Resource Power.

Positional Power

 Legitimate Power
The boss

 Reward Power
Bribery

 Coercive Power
Protection racket

 Resource Power
Controlling access

Personal Power

 Referent Power
I like you

 Expert Power
Special abilities

 Information Power
It's what you know

 Connection Power
... and who you know

POSITIONAL POWER
FROM YOUR STATUS IN THE WORLD

 Legitimate power, also called hierarchical power, comes from your place in a hierarchy and depends on other people's willingness to defer to your seniority. Tied to your role, it is most effective in autocratic organisations and when dealing with a crisis.

 Reward power comes from your ability to reward performance and offer inducements to secure it. The nature of the rewards that will be effective is the subject of many motivation theories. Rewards need not be material – recognition and praise are often highly valued.

 Coercive power is the evil twin of reward power, coming from your ability to make credible threats of punishment. While motivation based on fear is often successful, it is not sustainable in organisations where members have choice.

 Resource power – granting or withholding resources might be seen as reward or coercive power, but this addition to the list explains how relatively low-status administrators acquire power from their position as 'gate-keeper' to a valued resource.

PERSONAL POWER

FROM YOUR INVESTMENT IN YOURSELF

Referent power is true personal power. Often called charisma, it comes from how people view you: your integrity, personality, character, likeability, and rapport with others. This is the one power base which no one can strip from you, so is well worth investing in.

Expert power comes from your expertise gained from study, practice and experience. You are in control of this power but it takes constant investment to keep it up-to-date.

Information power comes from information you hold, or can access. It could be seen as a form of resource power, but in many sectors of today's economy, 'knowledge workers' access information themselves: power over resources is granted by the organisation.

Connection power comes from the people you know and your ability to deploy your network of relationships to good effect. You might harness their power positively (expertise, information) or negatively (coercion) to influence others.

LEADERSHIP & POWER

The link between leadership and power is a strong one and many of the theories of leadership can equally be framed as theories of power – how you lead depends upon what power bases you rely upon. Effective leaders often deploy different power bases at different times, according to need.

At its simplest, the way you wield power to get compliance can be appropriate or inappropriate. Appropriate use of power can be described as influence, while inappropriate use can be described as bullying.

Etzioni described how relative amounts of positional and personal power determine your leadership role.

HOW GOOD ARE POWER BASES?

Power bases offer a way to subdivide power. The real world is complex and we use multiple power bases. We could probably define an infinite number, based on the different resources available to us. The model does give us insights into how power works in organisations. Surveying people's power bases will help you to find assertive, respectful ways to deal with them. In the model, power requires dependency. By finding inter-dependencies, you can balance the power in your relationships with colleagues and collaborators – even with customers and suppliers.

This is how 'partnership working' functions. We can also see why it sometimes breaks down. Some organisations loudly espouse the value of partnership working while clinging to their power over you. When you do not grant them that power, they resort to ever less appropriate forms, which start to feel like bullying.

The relative importance of the bases is shifting. Some argue that the strength of positional power is diminishing. Information power is diminishing too, due to the ready access afforded by the internet.

8 POWER BASES

LEARN MORE

The literature on power bases is technical and contained in sociology texts and journals. A good general text that covers this topic well is:

- *Organizational Behaviour: An Introductory Text,* by Andrzej Huczynski and David Buchanan, Financial Times/Prentice Hall, 2006

Links in this pocketbook
Each power base links to other areas of management; eg referent power to the topics of influence and transformational leadership; and coercive and reward power to motivation. Direct links in this book are with:

- Vroom's **Expectancy Theory**, which will help you to gauge the effect of a potential reward on people's motivation
- McClelland's **Three Needs**, because one of our three needs is the need for power
- Adair's **Action Centred Leadership**, and Tannenbaum and Schmidt's **Leadership Continuum** both focus on how you can influence the performance of others, deploying a range of power bases
- Berne's **Transactional Analysis** will help you understand emotional power bases, and the games we play as a result of them

BEING EFFECTIVE AT WORK

9 Urgent versus important

10 OODA loop

BEING EFFECTIVE AT WORK

INTRODUCTION

Two models that will help you to be effective at work are about how to plan your time and how to deal with rapidly changing events. Together, they make a powerful resource:

Step 1: Plan how to use your time effectively by distinguishing what is Important from what is merely Urgent.

Step 2: Recognise that shift happens! The real world will not respect your plan so, to be successful, you need to be flexible and Boyd's OODA Loop gives you the ultimate model of flexible behaviour.

'...I have always found that plans are useless, but planning is indispensable.'

Dwight D. Eisenhower

THE PROBLEM

Have you ever spent the whole day working hard and still find yourself dissatisfied at the end of the day because you haven't achieved what you wanted to? Of course you have. Getting the most from your time is a constant problem we all face.

> 'Most things which are urgent are not important, and most things which are important are not urgent'
>
> Attributed to **Dwight D. Eisenhower**

Managing your time boils down to three problems:
1. Choosing what to do
2. Choosing when to do it
3. Getting it done in the time available

For most people, the problem with managing their time starts with number one. They feel overwhelmed by the amount that they feel they have to do. Choosing what to do can be broken into three questions:

1. Is it a *'want-to'*, a *'should-do'*, or a 'must-do'?
2. What if someone else did it?
3. What if it just didn't get done?

THE PROBLEM

Why are so few of us really good at managing our time? Firstly, we are not taught it. In childhood, people manage our time for us: when we leave school, we are expected to just figure it out. Secondly, it doesn't matter to us; until it really matters. We don't learn how to do it when time pressures are mild. Heavy time pressure somehow seems to creep up on us and catch us unawares.

Maybe you are someone who lives in the moment. Whatever you are doing now is so engrossing that your next meeting, your next task, even your next five minutes don't exist for you. You find it easy to get into what Mihaly Csikszentmihalyi describes as a 'flow state'. We can all enter 'flow' and it is captivating because it tends to be when we are happiest. So managing your time is essentially about managing your happiness.

The benefits of getting this right are tremendous:
- You can achieve more of the things that matter
- You can get the rewards of being someone who gets things done
- You can enjoy what you are doing in the process

9 URGENT VERSUS IMPORTANT

QUICK SUMMARY

President Eisenhower was the first to publicly distinguish between things that are urgent and things that are important, suggesting that most things are either one or the other. Author Stephen Covey put this insight at the core of the third of his seven habits of highly effective people: *'first things first'*. He argued that effective people prioritise things that are important, but not urgent.

Urgent and important tasks grab our attention and take top priority. When they mount up, we start to feel out of control.

Urgent but not important tasks are the interruptions, distractions and other people's priorities, which lead to busyness without the satisfaction of achievement – like a cheap hamburger that fills you up for a while but is not satisfying for long.

Not urgent and not important tasks are a waste of your time. These are trivial activities that displace valuable effort and rob you of productive time.

Not urgent but important tasks give you most value for your effort. They are investments in your future success and allow you to prioritise important tasks before they become urgent. Here you have control, so this is where to focus your quality time.

QUICK SUMMARY

'Important'
of great significance; having a big effect

'Urgent'
requiring immediate attention
The four combinations of urgency and importance each have their own characteristics.
It is the important but not urgent tasks that give you control over your time.

THE FOUR QUADRANTS

Urgent and important – The things that have to be done because the customer needs it now, or we're coming up to a deadline. These feel like crises and, while many people identify this as the quadrant to focus on, it is not. In this quadrant lies stress and eventual burnout. The secret lies elsewhere.

Urgent but not important – Constant interruptions and those endless meetings are all urgent, but how important are they, really? They may be important to someone else, but you need to say *'no'* more often or you will feel out of control; like a dinghy in a gale. You won't get any reward for saying *'yes'* indiscriminately.

Not urgent and not important – Trivial timewasters that help us avoid purposeful activity are neither important nor urgent. That gift catalogue you never buy from can't be important; if you don't look at it now, it'll still be on the table next week. Only waste time when you have time to waste; to do otherwise is irresponsible and will leave you feeling frustrated.

THE FOUR QUADRANTS

Not urgent but important – Here you can make real progress. In this quadrant you are investing in the future. Your tasks will have lasting consequence, even if there is little pressure to get them done now.

Planning, preparing and setting up systems or processes *can* wait; they are not urgent. But by investing time in them, you set yourself up for your future success. Likewise, building a strong working relationship with a client or colleague is an activity that will help you in the future, rather than now. Even reading and thinking fits in this category. Perhaps most surprisingly, so does resting, relaxing and doing things you enjoy. Recharging your batteries is an investment in yourself to prepare you for tomorrow.

To give yourself time for the important things, you must learn to **say no** to the unimportant. When you do focus on important activities while they are not urgent, you will prevent them from becoming urgent in the future, leaving you feeling in control of events, rather than controlled by them. Consequently, you will achieve a balanced workload and gain a sense of real productivity.

9 URGENT VERSUS IMPORTANT

FIRST THINGS FIRST

In Covey's *Seven Habits of Highly Effective People*, *'Put first things first'* is his third habit. He states that there is little we can do to manage time, but a lot we can do to manage ourselves. Putting first things first is about investing in activities that enhance your long-term purpose in life. If you know your purpose, you can set goals. Important activities are therefore activities that take you towards achieving your goals and thus succeeding in the roles you choose for yourself.

'The key is not to prioritize what's on your schedule, but to schedule your priorities.'

Stephen R Covey

In his later book, *First Things First*, Covey cites research into the amount of management time that companies spend in each of the four quadrants. Typical organisations spend around 15% of their time on 'not urgent but important tasks'. The highest performing organisations in the study, however, spend between 65% and 80% of their time here. This is largely time gained from the urgent but not important quadrant, where typical organisations spend 50% to 60% of their time, but the best spend only 15%. In these organisations, people clearly know how to **say no**, and feel confident to do so.

PRACTICAL TIME MANAGEMENT

The distinction between urgent and important will help you to determine what to do, though not when to do it, or how to get it done in the time. By understanding what you want to achieve, you can set yourself clear goals, which answer the question: *'what do I want?'*

In life, we tend to focus on the things we **must** do. The sense of obligation means we seldom enjoy them, however. We tend to feel guilty about not doing things we **should** do, because we certainly don't want to do them and, since they are not a *must*, we put them off. Fulfilment comes from focusing on the things we **want** to do. When you can link what you must do to what you want to do, you will no longer procrastinate or feel frustrated. When you confidently abandon the things you should do, knowing that you neither have to do them, nor want to do them, you will no longer feel burdened by them.

A great way to use the urgent-important matrix is to draw the grid on a large chart or whiteboard. Put all your 'to-dos' on sticky notes and place them where they belong. This will put the urgent but not important tasks in perspective, allow you to get on top of your urgent and important tasks, and leave time to prioritise the not urgent but important tasks in future.

HOW GOOD IS URGENT VERSUS IMPORTANT?

This will never be the sole solution to your time management problems. It does not address how to get things done, nor even how much time to allow. Its benefit is to focus you on **what** to do and, to a degree, why. It is entirely compatible with other time management tools and models, like:

- The four Ds: do, delegate, defer and drop
- Scheduling your most important tasks into your most productive time
- Task lists, prioritisation and sequencing

The key quadrant, not urgent but important, is sometimes misunderstood, and seen as self-indulgent. It is easy to see the value of things that are both urgent and important, but if it's not urgent, can't we put it off? You will find that not urgent but important often addresses the very same tasks; it just does so **before** they become urgent.

This is a simple but very powerful model. We all want to feel more productive. Eisenhower's insight teaches us that busyness for its own sake will not help us feel productive; we achieve more when we focus on what is important, rather than what is merely urgent.

LEARN MORE

Time management and personal effectiveness

- *The Seven Habits of Highly Effective People*, Stephen R Covey, Simon & Schuster Ltd, 2004
- *First Things First*, Stephen R Covey, A Roger Merrill & Rebecca R Merrill, Simon & Schuster Ltd, 1999
- *The Time Management Pocketbook*, Ian Fleming, Management Pocketbooks, 2003

More in this pocketbook

Delegating your work is an essential component of time management. The Tannenbaum and Schmidt **Leadership Continuum** will help you to delegate effectively. Your plan will soon be out of date. The next section introduces Boyd's **OODA Loop** to keep you focused on what is really happening and hence what is really important.

10 OODA LOOP

THE PROBLEM

How can you deal with rapidly changing events, stay ahead of them, and influence the outcomes? These are fundamental questions about being successful in any environment, whether you are:

'Events, dear boy, events.'

Attributed to **Prime Minister, Harold MacMillan,** on being asked what worried him most

- Competing against another person or group
- Negotiating with another organisation
- In a conflict situation – as participant or mediator
- Struggling to overcome personal adversity
- Implementing change, or managing uncertainty
- Seeking to learn from experience and be more successful in future

It would be a bold model-builder indeed that sought to develop a single model that could deal with such a wide range of circumstances. If such a model were to exist, it would be surprising if it were not well known. And yet …

10 OODA LOOP

QUICK SUMMARY

John Boyd's OODA Loop is a four-step cycle for making decisions in a changing environment. The power of the model comes from Boyd's observation that, when you speed up the rate at which you go around the loop, you increasingly gain control of the situation. The four steps are:

Observation – Use all of your senses and resources to gather information from the outside world.

Orientation – Figure out what your information is telling you, using a combination of analysis and intuitive responses.

Decision – Decide what you are going to do, in response to the situation.

Action – Take action, to test out your thinking.

Then observe the outcome of your action, review what you have learned, form a new decision and take action. If you move fast enough through this cycle, Boyd believed, you will control your situation.

QUICK SUMMARY

Boyd's OODA Loop
in its simplest form.

Boyd later clarified his
model. An intuitive
response to an Observation
can lead directly from
Orientation to Action,
without the need for a
conscious Decision. He also
noted that the Orientation and
Decision steps can influence
the act of Observation.

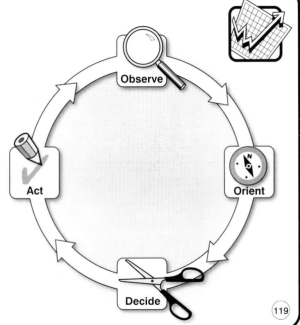

WHERE TO APPLY THIS MODEL

Negotiation – Here flexibility is essential for success. Keep alert for an opportunity opened up by your counter-party's tactics and quickly assess what it can mean to you. Having made your decision and acted on it, observe how the other person reacts.

Time management – How best to use your time, moment by moment. The OODA Loop suggests a fixed plan will let you down. Constant re-prioritisation based on actual progress and emerging priorities is a far better approach than a static schedule or 'to-do' list – especially in a fast moving operational environment.

Project management – No project plan survives first contact with the real world. As soon as you start to implement, your plan is out of date. So monitor what's going on, assess how it relates to your resources and objectives, then act decisively. This 'monitor and control cycle' is at the heart of project delivery.

Conflict management – Conflict can escalate out of control very quickly. If you are constantly alert to the subtle shifts in mood, and accommodate them accordingly, you can avert conflict easily. And if you are in conflict and want to win, the OODA Loop provides a framework for disruptive action that can give you the upper hand.

ORIENTATION: THE HEART OF THE OODA LOOP

The orientation step in the loop is where you combine new information with past experience, and where your heritage, traditions and knowledge work with deliberate analysis to develop options from which you can choose your next step.

Boyd stressed the importance of past experience in the orientation step, illustrating it as a dynamic interplay of influences. These influences filter our interpretation of what we observe. This will therefore not only influence our decisions and actions, but also what we observe. The constraints of our interpretation bias the way we observe the outside world. You may want to refer back to the NLP Model of Communication, earlier in this book.

> 'Orientation ... is the most important part of the OODA Loop since it shapes the way we observe, the way we decide, the way we act.'
>
> **Colonel John Boyd**

10 OODA LOOP

REFLECT, THEN DECIDE

This is a chapter title in Rudolph Giuliani's book, *Leadership*. In it, he considers the orientation step: *'I never make up my mind until I have to. Faced with any important decision, I always envision how each alternative will play out before I make it'*. Timothy Gallwey, in *The Inner Game of Work*, advocates the STOP Tool as *'the tool of all tools'*. This offers us a process for the orientation step of the OODA Loop.

Step back and separate yourself emotionally from the situation

Think: review all possible interpretations of what you have observed and your possible responses

Organise your thoughts

Proceed

Boyd tells us that the faster you can make your decision, the more control you will have. Giuliani says: *'Even though leaders should take as much time as available to make decisions, the process of making the decision should begin immediately.'* Boyd would go further and assert that, in fast-moving situations, a decision based on 80% of the information plus informed intuition will be better than waiting for all of the information and a thorough analysis.

ORIGINS OF THE OODA LOOP

Colonel John Boyd was a fighter pilot in the US Air Force, during the Korean War. Nicknamed '40 second Boyd', he had a rare ability to win aerial dog-fights by getting behind enemy planes. After the war, his experience and wide-ranging reading led him to become a widely respected military theorist, influencing a generation of military thinkers.

Boyd articulated the OODA Loop to describe military tactics and strategy. His principal argument was that if you could go around your OODA Loop faster than your adversary, you would get inside their decision cycle. This puts you in control and the encounter will feel to you like it is happening in slow motion.

This origin is probably why the OODA Loop is not better known. Also, while Boyd spoke to military audiences, he did not promote his thinking more widely, nor did he publish his writing. When business thinkers, like Joseph Bower and Thomas Hout, analysed the competitive performance of companies like Toyota and Honda, they found the OODA Loop a valuable model for how fast cycle times lead to competitive success.

HOW GOOD IS THE OODA LOOP?

A fair criticism of the OODA Loop is that it was not new when Boyd articulated it and that we have plenty of similar models already. Here are a few:

- **Shewhart Cycle** in quality control (also known as the Deming Cycle):
  Plan – Do – Check – Act, and the Six Sigma methods it inspired
- **Kolb Cycle** in learning: Concrete Experience – Observation and Reflection – Abstraction and Generalisation – Testing
- **Monitor and Control Loop** in project management: Deliver – Monitor – Control

Boyd was astonishingly well read. He synthesised many rich ideas into a simple model that was, for him, purely about warfare. The power of the OODA Loop is its universality. Like these other models, it emphasises continuous commitment over single intervention and the importance of speed for competitive advantage.

In a management context, you will want to be cautious how you introduce these ideas, given their military origin. The OODA Loop's real strength is in how you can adapt it endlessly, with different language and variations in its steps, to generate your own model for a very wide range of circumstances.

LEARN MORE

About the OODA Loop

Books about Boyd's work all focus on his military theory, so the best reference source is the internet. However, for related ideas, try:

- *Leadership*, Rudolph W Giuliani, Little Brown, 2002
- *Blink!*, Malcolm Gladwell, Allen Lane, 2005
- *The Inner Game of Work*, W Timothy Gallwey, Texere Publishing, 2003
- *Fast Cycle Capability for Competitive Power*, Joseph L Bower and Thomas M Hout, Harvard Business Review, November-December 1988

More in this pocketbook

- The **NLP Model of Communication** provides an alternative view of what goes on during the orientation step of the OODA Loop, identifying three important filters
- Like Boyd, Eisenhower was a military man, and the **Urgent-Important** distinction is a key element of your orientation strategy
- **John Adair** also started his career in the military, later training army officers. Many of his eight functions of leadership fit nicely into the OODA Loop

LAST WORD

How useful are models? Some would say they simply recapitulate common sense. But if they did not, how good could they be? Others would say that they inevitably over-simplify. But if they did not simplify, we'd have to make sense of all the complexity of the real world.

Instead, I take the view that models are the way that we, as humans, make sense of the world. We cannot help but make patterns from what we observe – that's how our brains are wired. Models are how we articulate these patterns.

How to reinstate the subtlety, without over-complicating, is the challenge that all model builders face. My solution has always been to look for the boundaries of each model's usefulness and then to seek connections to other related models or ideas. If my attempts to do this have given you a few insights or some new ideas to pursue, then I am happy.

About the Author

Dr Mike Clayton
Mike is a freelance speaker, advisor and trainer. He has worked with a wide range of organisations in the private, public and voluntary sectors, helping managers to improve their leadership and management skills. He specialises in leading and managing in times of change, where he can apply his experience of and passion for project and change management.

He has found models a useful way of collating and explaining his experiences, across 20 years of consulting, training and coaching. He has been a Senior Manager at Deloitte and is a Director of Kent Trainers.

Contact
You can contact Mike at:
The Old Chapel House, 20A Pound Hill, Alresford, Hampshire, SO24 9BW.
Tel: 01962 736019 E-mail: mike@thoughtscape.net

ORDER FORM

Your details

Name _____

Position _____

Company _____

Address _____

_____

_____

Telephone _____

Fax _____

E-mail _____

VAT No. (EC companies) _____

Your Order Ref _____

Please send me:

	No. copies
The Management Models Pocketbook	☐
The _____ Pocketbook	☐
The _____ Pocketbook	☐
The _____ Pocketbook	☐

Order by Post
MANAGEMENT
POCKETBOOKS LTD
LAUREL HOUSE, STATION APPROACH,
ALRESFORD, HAMPSHIRE SO24 9JH UK
Order by Phone, Fax or Internet
Telephone: +44 (0)1962 735573
Facsimile: +44 (0)1962 733637
E-mail: sales@pocketbook.co.uk
Web: www.pocketbook.co.uk

Customers in USA should contact:
Management Pocketbooks
2427 Bond Street, University Park, IL 60466
Telephone: 866 620 6944 Facsimile: 708 534 7803
E-mail: mp.orders@ware-pak.com
Web: www.managementpocketbooks.com